Autism Perspectives

Susan Louise Peterson

Copyright Notice

Autism Perspectives. Copyright © 2015 by Susan Louise Peterson All rights reserved. No part of this book may be used or reproduced in any manner whatsoever without written permission of the publisher.

Table of Contents

Preface..iv
Prologue v
Acknowledgements..vi
Introduction..vii
CHAPTER 1 : Benefits of a Multi-Team Autism Assessment............1
CHAPTER 2 : The Parent & the Autism Referral Process 4
CHAPTER 3 : Why Autism is Confusing to Parents..........................7
CHAPTER 4: Mistaken Mannerism of Autism 10
CHAPTER 5: Autism-Obvious Symptoms or
        Questionable Signs 13
CHAPTER 6: A Single Trait of Autism 16
CHAPTER 7: Cultural Factors that Could Impact an Autism
        Eligibility 19
CHAPTER 8: Understanding Autism Educational
        Placement...22
CHAPTER 9: What are Professionals Observing for
        Autism Signs?...25
CHAPTER 10: What Distinguishes Whether a Child has
        Autism or Developmental Delays?..............................28
CHAPTER 11: Five Rituals of Possible Autism...............................31
CHAPTER 12: Five Autism Resources for Parents.........................34
Recommended Reading for Autism 38
Afterword..40

Preface

Parents are super busy and sometimes they need information in small pieces. This book is written in twelve mini chapters on a variety of topics related to autism.

There are chapters on topics such as the referral process, multi-team assessments, confusion, traits and mannerisms of autism, autism signs and symptoms, cultural factors related to autism, autism educational placement, rituals and autism resources for parents. ***Autism Perspectives*** contains small pieces of information that can provide a nice beginning point for parents in their journey to guide their child's educational path.

Prologue

I have written other books on autism, but this small book is simply a collection of short mini articles to explore many of the autism topics that parents struggle with in raising children with autism. The mass amount of information on autism can confuse parents and sometimes this information just needs to be presented in an easy to understand approach. It is my hope that parents can find these articles useful in their journey to find answers about autism.

Acknowledgements

I really want to thank the education and clinic professionals who have given me many perspectives about autism and other conditions that impact young children. When I first started working in education, I thought I knew a few things about autism, but the professionals I have worked with have really opened my eyes from their fabulous training and educational experiences. These wonderful professional friendships certainly have impacted my perspectives about autism.

I want to thank my husband and children for being understanding and supportive in my writing career. They have always given me space to pursue my dream of writing and my love of working with young children. I am really blessed with a wonderful family and great kids.

Introduction

I wrote this short book, ***Autism Perspectives*** to explore twelve mini topics related to the field of autism for parents. Parents are often hurried and struggle with time management so they need information that comes in smaller pieces to spark their ideas and ask questions about the autism concerns they have for their children. The information is presented in a practical way so that parents can understand some of the process for autism assessments and autism referrals.

CHAPTER 1

Benefits of a Multi-Team Autism Assessment

As a school psychologist, my favorite type of assessment for autism and developmental delays is definitely a multi-team assessment. Parents can really benefit from more than one professional to notice, watch or observe different aspects of the child's communication and behavior. These varied observations can provide feedback on the child from various people who have worked with or observed different characteristics or patterns of communication the child may present related to autism. School districts may vary in the team members making a multi-team assessment, but the teams could include teachers (regular or special education), a speech therapist, a school psychologist, a school nurse and possibly a physical or occupational therapist if warranted. The speech therapist, for example can play a vital role in understanding the child's pragmatic communication and looking at communication in a social or practical way.

There is a real disadvantage of using a single person assessment for autism. The professional making the autism assessment may have had limited experiences working with young children with developmental delays and autism concerns. A single professional may not have adequate training in the field of autism. It is important to note that one professional may be competent and have many experiences working with young children who have autism characteristics, but often a parent doesn't know for sure about the professional conducting the assessment, making an autism diagnosis or determining an autism educational eligibility. If the one professional is well trained the parent may get some helpful information about the child related to autism, but if the professional is poorly trained and has limited experiences working with children, the information related to autism and developmental delays can be confusing and overwhelming for parents. It is so important to get to get a variety of viewpoints from professionals and this can easily be done with a multi-team autism assessment.

A multi-team assessment can be much broader than just an assessment in the office. It could include a home observation to see how the child reacts to social situations or communication experiences in a familiar setting. Sometimes preschool observations are used to watch how the child interacts in play experiences with other children in structured or unstructured social situations. The multi-team assessment is truly beneficial in providing parents with lots of detailed information on the child from different angles given by professionals with different perspectives. The multi-team assessment can be used to help parents in future educational planning for the child with possible autism, developmental delays or other disorders and conditions.

CHAPTER 2

The Parent & the Autism Referral Process

When a parent starts having concerns that a child may have autism or developmental delays he or she may start calling agencies or the school district to find out about the referral process. This may take some time as the parent may need to call a few phone numbers to find the appropriate office that takes a referral for an autism assessment. The referral itself can come from a variety of scenarios. Sometimes the parents themselves or a relative in the family notices possible autism traits so the parents either calls on their own or is encouraged to call for testing from family members. However, a referral can come from an early childhood specialist or therapist who has been working with the child. A visit to the school for an older child may get a suggestion from school staff to test the younger child if any unusual behaviors or possible delays are noticed. Sometimes a child attends a day care center or preschool and the staff worker or preschool teacher notices certain behaviors that signal a red flag or possibility of autism. A doctor may mention to the parent that autism is a possibility and encourage further school district testing.

If a parent calls the school district for a referral there may be a brief phone interview to ask the parent questions about their concerns for the child. These questions help the school district clinic determine if the referral question is related to autism, health concerns, speech issues, developmental delays or other conditions. Once a date is set for testing, a more formal intake is done to collect additional information and get the testing and assessment started. Parents must be aware that the process will take some time and many districts have long waiting lists just to get in the door for the initial autism referral and assessment.

A couple of hints for parents related to the autism referral process include starting early (don't put this off), never skip appointments (it will delay the process) and try not to reschedule or there will be even more delays. Don't forget to listen to the professionals making the assessment. Although, you may have a lot of knowledge about your child take time to listen to the experienced professionals and see what points of view they have about your child and the referral and assessment process. You are welcome in the referral and assessment process to ask questions, seek clarification and request more of an explanation on areas that seem unclear or confusing. On a side note, many parents really gain a lot of information about their children as they go through this referral and testing process.

CHAPTER 3

Why Autism is Confusing to Parents

Many parents will mention that they are totally confused about autism. This confusion can come from three areas. First, confusion about autism stems from the large amount of autism information available on websites, news services, television and social media. The parent starts hearing so many different ideas about autism that he or she gets confused about what autism means or represents. A relative or family member can have concerns that a child may have autism and share it with the parent. A parent taking a college class may hear a lecture on autism and notice that many characteristics describe his or her own child. It can seem easy at first because the child does have a few symptoms that could possibly be autism. However, many parents are unaware of the crossover between symptoms of autism with other disorders or possible developmental delays. The parent may need help from professionals to sort out what certain characteristics or traits are more prominent in the child.

The second area of the confusion happens when the parent starts asking questions about autism. Autism is often seen as a controversial disorder so parents start hearing different angles or viewpoints about the disorder. A parent may ask the same question to a medical doctor, a counselor, a school psychologist or child development specialist and get totally different answers from the professionals about autism. The differing answers are sometimes the result of the different training experiences of the professionals.

Finally, a third area of confusion is when the parents need to make decisions about the child's educational program and then autism information can be even more confusing for parents. The parent may be faced with a decision as to a suitable educational program for the child. The parent can get confused about all the terms of what entails a self-contained program, a community based type of program or a more intensive specialized autism program. Sometimes autism terms are difficult for parents who are unfamiliar with special education or the educational programs where they live.

Parents must then sort through all this information and it can be a painful process. In this journey, the parent may discover the child has autism, has some characteristics of autism, does not have autism or simply has some developmental delays that need intervention, support and therapy. A parent must focus on his or her own child to get a full picture of the unique characteristics of the child and know what concerns or limitations need to be addressed related to autism concerns.

CHAPTER 4

Mistaken Mannerism of Autism

A parent may sometimes mistake one mannerism or concern of the child as definitely being autism. A deficit area may be a sign or an indication of autism, but could also indicate another type of condition or possible delay. Parents may need to work with professionals to see the broad picture of the child and how the sign or mannerism relates to the child's ability to communicate and socially interact with others. Some children are just a little 'atypical' or unusual in their mannerisms, but this could be a sign of many different things. I think of a child who is very gifted and who thinks outside of the box. This child may overly examine a toy to the point of being excessive, but a good professional would spot this child has higher cognitive abilities or a strong curiosity of an object, rather than having autism.

Another example might be a child who is not speaking by age three and he or she would have a delay in the communication area. A child with autism who is not speaking also has a delay or deficit in communication. Professionals working with the child will then start observing the child's 'intent' or willingness to communicate with others. The speech therapist may look to see if the child shows a desire to communicate with others, but just has a limited vocabulary to express him or herself. On the other hand, a child with autism may be using some words, but in a more repetitive way, rather than communicating wants, needs or desires.

The professional is watching if the language is directed to others or if the child is unresponsive or avoiding social interaction. If the child is avoiding social interaction by not speaking, the professional will look to see if the avoidance is willful, whether the child understands the request or whether the child engages with others in some way. However, if the child's communication presented as unresponsive, withdrawn and lacking 'intent' to reach out to others then there would be more reason to explore the area of autism. Professionals tend to look at the whole picture of the child and don't usually focus an entire assessment on one unusual, atypical or different mannerism. Parents and professionals would not want to mistake a single unusual mannerism of the child with a child who has autism with an abundance of characteristics or deficits in the socialization and or communication areas.

CHAPTER 5

Autism-Obvious Symptoms or Questionable Signs

Children with possible autism may present in two ways. There are some children who have clear cut or obvious signs of autism. This may be a kid that when people are around him or her notice that there is something different or unusual about the child. It could be the parents or a relative having a feeling that the child may have autism. The preschool educator or developmental specialist may document or start to suspect signs of autism while observing the child in the home setting. A doctor may note characteristics or traits of autism in his or her medical report School district employees may encourage a parent to get a younger sibling of an older child who is attending the local elementary school to be tested for autism. Often these cases of autism are more clear cut because the symptoms of autism are obvious and observed more frequently by different people. There is not a lot of discussion or disagreement of the characteristics these children present because these children may play by themselves and stay away from other children even when there are many children and activities around them.

There is also a second type of child that presents with more questionable signs of autism. These are much harder cases for professionals to determine if a child has developmental delays or possible autism. Experienced preschool teachers may want to work with the child to see if he or she will start warming up and gaining more skills to participate and interact in the preschool setting. Since children in early childhood programs can make rapid changes related to socialization and communication there is a definite benefit in putting a child in a preschool to look for obvious symptoms and questionable signs related to autism. This can also provide parents with valuable information to see if the child is meeting developmental milestones or has delays.

Professionals may doubt autism because the child does certain things very appropriately and at other times presents with inconsistent or unpredictable types of responses to requests. When there are doubts and questions about whether the child has autism there is a need to delve deeper for more information on the child's reactions, responses, capabilities and skill development related to the communication and socialization areas. Additional consultation with outside specialists related to behavior, sensory, eating or academic issues may be needed to collect more information on the child.

CHAPTER 6

A Single Trait of Autism

Parents sometimes ask this question 'if the child has one trait of autism does that mean he or she definitely has autism?' This is where I am cautious about making a child eligible for autism based on a single trait. Take for example, toe walking which some parents report as a trait for possible autism. Toe walking is a characteristic of autism, but it may also be related to other disorders. Therefore, the educational team would not want to make a decision based on a single trait or characteristic. This would not do justice in fully describing the child and it would base an eligibility decision on very limited information about the child.

An early childhood assessment for autism may include many things. Often an assessment will look at the child's cognitive abilities, preschool readiness skills, daily living skills, motor skills, socialization skills and communication skills. A speech evaluation as part of the autism assessment can provide valuable information about how a child communicates with others and reaches out socially with language. An early childhood autism assessment not only includes testing instruments, but also includes notes from the professional's observation of the child.

If a person looks at autism from just one trait, there is a likelihood that other traits (which may be appropriate or inappropriate) are overlooked in the child. I have also noticed that some professionals are a little more skillful than others in their ability to bring a child out of shyness, help a child warm up to a new situation and get the child to communicate his or her wants or needs (especially with interesting toys). A single trait may be noticed by one professional, but not observed at all by other professionals. This is the time when professionals must communicate information with each other to see if these differences require further observation or testing.

The professionals working with the child should collect enough information to make a well documented decision about autism. Parents should think about autism in relation to a child's communication and socialization deficits and not only on one unusual, atypical or quirky behavior or trait. Multi-team assessments are usually looking for an abundance of autism characteristics in the child and not just one specific trait. When an eligibility of autism is based on a single trait it provides a very limited picture of the child. Autism is a spectrum type of disorder that entails a broad range of characteristics and traits.

CHAPTER 7

Cultural Factors that Could Impact an Autism Eligibility

There are many cultural factors that could impact whether a child is delayed, has autism or possibly another condition. These cultural factors could be such things as a family custom, a second language issue or a cultural difference that may impact how a child presents to an educational team. A good example of this would be a team looking at whether a child plays with toys appropriately. In one instance a child may have just arrived to a new country and has not had many toys. The child is fearful of electronic or musical toys in part because he or she has never been around these types of toys. As a result, the child may withdraw or close down when these types of toys are presented. On the surface, a professional may almost suspect the child has some autism characteristics. However, once the family social and cultural history is taken and the transitions to a new country are noted a different angle is approached. The child then would probably be viewed in the context of the change and playing with the toys inappropriately would be part of a cultural difference and lack of play experiences with certain types of toys rather than an autism characteristic.

Sometimes a cultural factor considered as autism is actually related to a cultural custom. If there is an expectation in one culture that a child should make eye contact and the child does not make eye contact a professional might say the child has a characteristic of autism. Certainly, some children with autism concerns do avoid eye contact or look away from social contacts. However, some cultural groups avoid direct eye contact or use eye contact for only limited periods or a short duration of time. A professional will sometimes notice that a parent displays a similar characteristic of the child. The child may not make eye contact, but other family members may not make a lot of eye contact either or speak with their eyes turned away from a speaker. The professional should strive not to confuse a cultural factor or custom with a child who has significant deficits in social interaction or communication. Observations of the child as well as discussions with the parent related to culture can help professionals have a greater understanding of cultural factors and family customs that sometimes seem to be related to autism, but are actually related to the culture and lifestyle of the family.

CHAPTER 8

Understanding Autism Educational Placement

Autism educational placement is done after the child has been found with an autism eligibility. In most school districts a multidisciplinary team of school staff members will review the results of the child's testing and evaluation with the parents. The team will often explain to the parents what special education options are available to children in the school district. The staff will then help the parents to see what type of program might be best suited for the child based upon the results of the testing, assessments and observations. Each special education program will vary in regards to class size, the number of staff working with the child, the amount of time provided for support and direct assessment with the child. Some children have significant medical needs as well and may require a home based program so that medical care can be facilitated with the educational needs of the child. Some children with autism may need home support for a while and then are able to make a transition to a school setting. The educational team will work with the parent to make sure supports are in place if the school needs to provide medical care, special accommodations, dieting restrictions, allergy alerts or anything else that will help the child succeed in the school setting.

The area of autism educational placement draws many questions from parents in the educational assessment process. I think placement really revolves around both the skills and abilities of the child as well as the deficits or delays of the child. Some children have multiple or severe delays and need more intensive intervention in a full day specialized autism program. Other children with autism may be placed in a half day program with children who have developmental delays. Yet other children are placed in a type of half and half program where the child may spend half the day in a specialized autism program and the other half in regular education program with special education support. This is often done to see if the child would be able to make a transition to a least restrictive type of setting. There are also students with autism who can handle a full day regular education program who only need monitoring or consultation from a special education teacher. I think since each child is unique and has individual issues autism placement can be approached from a number of creative angles in diverse school districts and educational programs.

CHAPTER 9

What are Professionals Observing for Autism Signs?

Professionals are quite varied in their ideas about autism so they could be observing different things depending on their fields of study and levels of training in the area of autism. I do think there are some general things that many professionals may be observing as they work with the child. The first one most professionals notice is how the child presents him or herself in an unfamiliar setting. The professional is seeing how the child adapts to new people, changing locations and new requests. There are also observations of how the child transitions from one room to another. The professional may see if the child tantrums when making a change, separates easily from the parent or is extremely clingy with the parent. Team members will talk and see how the child was with different people on the team. For example, did the child cry in the first part of the assessment in the nurse's office, but then warm up later and participate in the speech therapy assessment. This is a way to see if the child is responding across different settings and with a variety of people.

Sometimes additional observations are needed to get a better picture of the child with possible autism signs. There are times when school psychologists or team members change their opinions about whether a child has autism based on an observation. A child may appear unresponsive during an office visit and then present as a much more social child when observed in a preschool setting. For instance, a preschool observation is great for watching how the child interacts with same age children and responds to a preschool teacher's requests. When a young child exhibits a showing behavior by taking a toy to the teacher or giving a toy to another child, the professional can get a better picture of the child's intent to communicate and reach out to others. Professionals want to observe if the child who is suspected of having autism is presenting certain behaviors or characteristics in many settings or just in limited situations with certain people.

These professional observations can help answer many parenting questions about possible autism and these observations can help give expanded information to the parents and professionals making decisions about possible autism and delays. Many of these observations are presented to parents during the school district eligibility meeting and in the eligibility report that is given to the parents.

CHAPTER 10

What Distinguishes Whether a Child has Autism or Developmental Delays?

There are times when a parent naturally assumes that if a child is not doing the same thing as his cousin he must have autism. Parents are sometimes not familiar that there are many types of developmental delays that might better describe a child than autism, For instance, the child may have a communication delay and use very few words to talk to others. A child could also be delayed in his or her cognitive abilities, preschool readiness skills, motor, daily living or socialization skills. Parents should start early to obtain an early childhood assessment because interventions to help young children tend to be more successful when they are started earlier. If a parent waits until the child is five years old to mention his or her concerns, the child has already missed a lot of educational support from developmental specialists, speech therapists, preschool early childhood programs and other professionals that could have been working with the child. Parents have often commented to me that they have seem positive changes in children with autism from the early childhood interventions. An early childhood assessment would identify if a child has delays or just typical patterns of development. If autism concerns are noted by the parent then staff observation will be made in the assessment and rating scales or checklists may be used to identify autism characteristics or the frequency of behaviors or traits related to autism.

What comes to mind when I think of the assessment process for a child is whether the child has an 'abundance of characteristics' that fall in the area of autism. When a child does only one or two atypical or quirky things, but then presents with many appropriate or typical behaviors in their social exchanges and communication responses, I would probably lean more toward developmental delays. If the child presents with an abundant or many characteristics that show patterns or deficits in communication, social interaction, stereotyped (e.g. ritual like or repetitive) behaviors and restricted interests, I tend to lean more toward a possible autism eligibility. However, I will say there can be other issues such as second language issues, the mental illness and medical/social history of the family and genetic concerns that would be worthy to look at in the assessment process. I always try to emphasize that we sometimes need to step back and really look at the child's delays and background before we immediately jump to the autism eligibility.

CHAPTER 11

Five Rituals of Possible Autism

Parents may notice the first signs of possible autism when a child shows ritual types of behaviors. Here are five rituals parents may take note of:

Over Focused on Grouping Objects

Even though young children are encouraged to sort and put objects in groups for categorization, children with autism signs tend to make a ritual out of grouping objects together as they become over focused on a particular toy or types of toys. These children do not want anyone else to mess up or disturb the objects that have been carefully put in a group. A child may show anxious behavior when a particular toy or object in a group is slightly moved or altered.

Overly Possessive of Toys or Objects

Young children can become so possessive of household objects that no one else can touch or bother those objects without an outburst from the child. Parents once told me their child lined up wooden spoons and the child became so possessive of the wooden spoons that no one else in the house could touch those wooden spoons.

Restricted Interest in One Type of Toy or Object

Parents quickly notice when a child has a variety of toys, but shows a restricted interest in only one toy or object. This is different than showing a preference for a toy, but then playing with a variety of toys. When a child is so restricted in his or her interest of a toy object there seems to be an abnormal preoccupation of the toy and rituals often start to develop in the child's play practices.

Overly Interested in the Order of Toys or Objects

Parents will really notice that a child can have a very ritualistic and precise order of play with toys or objects. It may start out with lining up toy cars, however some children (with or without autism) may line up cars. Sometimes children will line up toys or objects without using objects for their intended purposes. A child with possible autism concerns may line up crayons neatly side by side or take all of the wrappers off all of the crayons while lining them in a pattern, but never actually pick up crayons to color or draw a picture.

Inflexibility to Change

A child may show ritualistic signs of possible autism by being inflexible to any change or disruption of an item, group of objects or even a movement pattern of an object that is repeated. If the object or pattern of movement is interrupted that child may show tantrum behavior, become distraught or upset from the change.

In summary, ritual types of behavior will vary in children. A child may be doing a ritual like or repetitive behavior to communicate a need (that people around him or her do not understand). Children will vary in the type of ritual that stresses one child and may not bother another child. In the same way, a ritual may calm or provide comfort for one child and not be of interest to another child.

CHAPTER 12

Five Autism Resources for Parents

When parents suspect their child may have autism there is an array of resources to help them. Many of these resources and services can be found in five major categories.

Diagnostic Resources

Parents will probably be looking into diagnostic services to verify if the child has autism or possible developmental delays. Diagnostic resources can take many directions. This might include a psychological assessment from a private practice psychologist or neuropsychologist as well as a medical diagnosis of autism from a physician. School districts also provide multi-team assessments of young children for delays and possible autism. A comprehensive assessment can provide the parents with lots of feedback and information about the child's development.

Parent Resources

Parenting resources and services for autism are plentiful for parents in lots of communities. Many autism organizations provide parents with general information about autism as well as how a child with autism can live an enriching life through school and community experiences. Parents can receive information on support groups and people in the community to provide networks of help and encouragement. A good parent resource for many families is called respite care which gives parents a short break to balance family responsibilities and lessen stress on family members.

Advocacy Resources

Advocacy resources for autism are utilized by some parents and not others. A parent may use a special education advocate to consult with during an eligibility or individualized education program (IEP) meeting. An advocate may help answer legal questions or be familiar with state codes or guidelines that could impact a child's educational program. However, advocacy may include broader elements of autism. Young students with autism may be taught self-advocacy skills to speak out for themselves and their needs. Advocacy can also include fundraising, speaking at political rallies or advocating for political or educational changes to inform the community about the needs of individuals with autism.

Therapeutic Resources

There are many therapeutic types of resources for families dealing with autism. Some of these therapeutic approaches are covered by insurance and government programs, while other therapeutic resources are not covered and families must pay their own expenses. There are a broad range of therapeutic resources such as behavior therapy, social skills training, psychiatric medications, individualized intervention programs, private speech, occupational and physical therapy, individual and group therapy sessions, self esteem programs, movement, massage, aquatic and hippo therapy and diet and nutrition based therapies, as well as a number of other programs. The important thing to note is that some therapeutic resources are more established with research to support the approaches and other therapies have limited research and evidence to know the effectiveness of the therapy.

Education Resources

Education resources for families start young and can follow the child through adulthood. Early intervention services in many communities start at birth and go to around three years old. A young child then can make a transition to the public schools for preschool programs that begin several years before Kindergarten. Individualized education programs can be developed through high school and the early adult years. Some parents choose to home school or go to a specialized private school with individualized types of curriculum. Parents can also use educational resources from summer camps, after school programs, adaptive sports, tutoring services, vocational training and transition types of programs. Educational resources can be tailored to the unique needs of the individual with autism.

Autism resources can really help direct parents to programs that provide specific services for the particular needs of their children.

Recommended Reading for Autism

Peterson, S. (2013). *Is my child autistic or delayed?*

Is My Child Autistic or Delayed? is a book geared to help parents and professionals examine autism concerns and developmental delays in children. The book is both parent and professional friendly written in an easy style to understand language. It would also benefit college students learning to work with parents and early childhood students with delays and autism concerns.
The school psychologist perspective is presented throughout the book.

Is My Child Autistic or Delayed? is a fabulous resource for parents (and professionals) beginning the process of an educational assessment for possible autism consideration and developmental delays.

Is My Child Autistic or Delayed? is available in both print and ebook versions and was selected for the **Gold Winner in the 2014 eLit Awards**, a **Silver Winner in the 2013 Global Ebook Awards** program and the **2014 West Mountain Regional Reader Views Book** awards program.

Peterson, S, (2014). *Questionable Autism*
The book *Questionable Autism* is directed into opening discussions about a variety of autism issues from many viewpoints. Looking at professional, parenting, research and testing issues numerous questions are developed to consider the broad impact of autism topics for both parents and professionals across settings. Author Susan Louise Peterson shares her experiences as an educator and school psychologist in the early childhood field into a discussion of some of the major issues impacting the field of autism. *Questionable Autism* is practical and includes many real world examples and experiences related to

parenting topics, field issues and general practices in the area of autism. ***Questionable Autism*** is focused on opening the doors for broader discussions of many issues in the field autism.

Peterson, S. (2015). *Possible Autism*

Parents have so many practical issues and concerns for their children that they have trouble getting through much of the information on autism, delays and disorders. Susan Louise Peterson, award winning autism author and school psychologist helps parents look at a number of practical parent issues from a school psychologist's point of view. ***Possible Autism*** covers autism attributes, features, connections, aspects and autism indicators on a broad range of topics. The goal of the book is to help parents explore if the parent issue presented may possibly be an autism characteristic or if other delays and possibilities could be considered.

Afterword

Even though I have training and experience as a school psychologist for many years in a school district I am well aware of the changing nature of the issues that impact both the child with autism and the parent caring for the child with autism. Not only are there differences in how each professional views the condition of a child there are also a number of legal and policy changes that impact how programs are administered for a child with autism. One professional may have an approach the works well with a child who has autism, but on a different day when a professional has another approach the child may respond in a totally different way. ***Autism Perspectives*** was written to share a few mini articles that could help parents clarify some of the issues impacting young children with autism. ***Autism Perspectives*** is just a starting point to help parents see some of the issues that can impact a child with autism.

www.ingramcontent.com/pod-product-compliance
Lightning Source LLC
Chambersburg PA
CBHW021137300426
44113CB00006B/460